W9-BMT-719

CRAFT BOX

Craft Like

THE TUDORS

Jillian Powell

PowerKiDS press

Published in 2018 by **The Rosen Publishing Group, Inc.**
29 East 21st Street, New York, NY 10010

Cataloging-in-Publication Data
Names: Powell, Jillian.
Title: Craft like the Tudors / Jillian Powell.
Description: New York : Powerkids Press, 2018. | Series: Craft box | Includes index.
Identifiers: ISBN 9781499433715 (pbk.) | ISBN 9781499433685 (library bound) | ISBN 9781499433609 (6 pack)
Subjects: LCSH: Great Britain--History--Tudors, 1485-1603--Juvenile literature. | England--Civilization--
   16th century--Juvenile literature. | Handicraft--Juvenile literature.
Classification: LCC DA315.P68 2018 | DDC 942.05--dc23

Editor: Elizabeth Brent
Designer: Rocket Design (East Anglia) Ltd
Craft stylist: Annalees Lim
Photographer: Simon Pask, N1 Studios

Picture acknowledgments: All step-by-step craft photography: Simon Pask, N1 Studios; images
used throughout for creative graphics: Shutterstock with the exception of p5, tr iStock photo.

Manufactured in China
CPSIA Compliance Information: Batch #BS17PK: For Further Information contact
Rosen Publishing, New York, New York at 1-800-237-9932

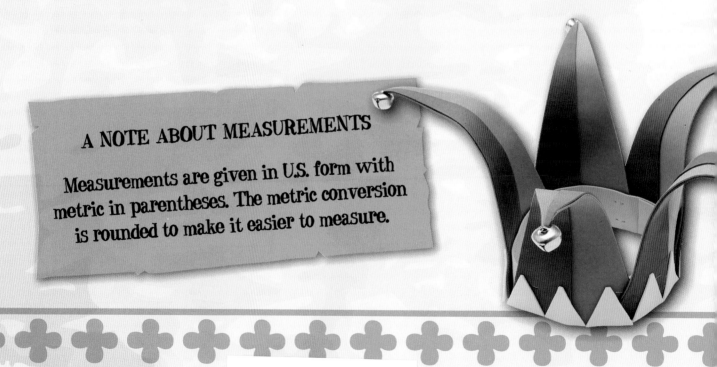

A NOTE ABOUT MEASUREMENTS

Measurements are given in U.S. form with metric in parentheses. The metric conversion is rounded to make it easier to measure.

Contents

the Tudors

The Tudor family ruled England and Wales for more than 100 years. Tudor kings and queens, such as King Henry VIII and Queen Elizabeth I, are some of the most famous **monarchs** in British history.

The Tudor monarchs **reigned** from 1485–1603 CE.

In Tudor times, cities and towns grew as houses, shops, schools, and theaters were built for a growing population. The wealthy paid artists to paint their **portraits**, and writers, including William Shakespeare, to write plays for theaters. Tudor ships sailed around the world, exploring new lands and bringing back spices, silks, and plants such as potatoes and tobacco. New **navigation** tools and skills helped explorers to map lands they had never been to before, like America.

Tudor craftsmen were skilled at working with materials such as wood, metals, gems, and leather. Each group of craftsmen were members of a **guild**, like modern trade unions.

Some craftsmen worked as traveling journeymen, others in workshops. Big houses, colleges, and churches often had their own workshops with **apprentices** and **journeymen** working under a master craftsman.

The buildings and objects they made can tell us a lot about the way people lived in Tudor times: the clothes they wore, how they decorated their homes, and the games they played. They can also inspire you to make some Tudor crafts of your own!

make a
Tudor rose

The Tudor rose is a symbol of the union between two families, the Lancasters and the Yorks. When King Henry VII married Elizabeth of York, the white rose of York and the red rose of Lancaster were joined to represent the new royal family: the Tudors.

You will need:

+ Colored felt
+ Marker
+ Ruler
+ Scissors
+ Felt glue
+ Pin
+ Needle and thread

1 Draw a star with five points, measuring about 3 inches (8 cm) across, onto a piece of green felt and cut it out.

2 Cut out a piece of red felt in the shape of a flower with five petals. Glue it on top of the green felt, so that the five green points are just showing.

3 Cut a smaller flower shape with five petals from white felt and glue this in the middle of the red flower.

4

Cut a circle of yellow felt big enough to fill the center of the white flower. Glue the yellow circle onto the middle of the white rose.

5

Glue the pin to the back off the green felt. Gently press down, then allow to dry.

Did you know ...
Tudor roses appear on the UK's royal coat of arms.

make a
Masquerade mask

Masquerade balls were popular in Tudor times. Guests wore masks to hide their identities. The fashion for wearing masks came from **medieval** entertainers called mummers, and from Italian mask **carnivals.**

You will need:
+ Pencil
+ Card stock
+ Scissors
+ Ruler
+ Marker
+ Acrylic paints
+ Brushes
+ Craft stick
+ Feathers
+ Glue or tape
+ Curly wrapping ribbon
+ Glitter glue or sequins

1 Draw a mask shape onto the card stock and cut it out. Mark the eyeholes and cut them out.

2 Use the pencil and ruler to mark out areas you want to paint in different colors, and then go over these lines using the marker. Color some of the sections in black. Make sure your design is **symmetrical.**

3 Paint the remaining sections using acrylic paints.

4 Paint the craft stick using acrylic paints and glue or tape it to the back of the mask.

5 Glue or tape feathers to the top of the mask, and curly ribbon to the sides of the mask.

6 Use glitter glue or sequins to decorate your mask.

Did you know...
Masks were worn by actors in musicals called masques and mummeries.

make a Jester's crown

Jesters were popular entertainers on the streets and in the **Royal Court** in Tudor times. They acted foolishly, sang funny songs, and told jokes. They wore colorful costumes and hats like floppy crowns that were decorated with bells.

You will need:

+ Craft foam in three or more colors
+ Scissors
+ Fabric glue and stapler
+ Small craft bells
+ Ruler
+ Sequins/fake gems

1 Cut a strip of craft foam 2 inches (5 cm) wide and long enough to fit around your head, plus an extra inch (3 cm). Staple the ends together to form a band.

2 Cut ten triangles of craft foam in different colors. Cut five of the triangles in half, and then glue one half-triangle to the front of each whole triangle and one to the back on the opposite side. Leave to dry.

3 Glue or staple the triangles to the band, lining up the base of each triangle with the bottom of the band. Space the triangles to cover the band.

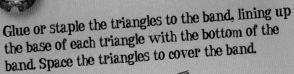
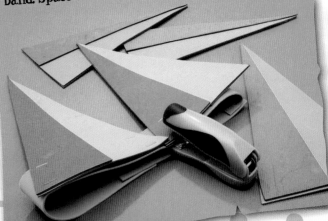

4 Glue a craft bell to the pointed end of each triangle.

5 Decorate the band with foam shapes, sequins, or fake gems.

Did you know ...
Tudor street entertainers included acrobats, jugglers, and tightrope walkers.

make a
Jester's stick

Jesters' costumes made them look like comical kings. They carried sticks shaped like royal **scepters**, with bells to shake as they told jokes or did pranks to amuse and entertain the Royal Court.

1 Push one end of the stick into the Styrofoam ball and glue in place.

2 Paint the ball and craft stick or dowel using acrylic paints. Allow them to dry.

3 Draw two circles, 2 inches (5 cm) and 5 inches (13 cm) in diameter, on foam or construction paper and cut them out.

4 Cut the big circle into a flower shape to make a collar. Then push the collar onto the stick beneath the ball.

5 Cut six pieces of ribbon of different lengths up to 5 inches (13 cm) long. Thread a craft bell onto the end of each and tie a knot to hold it on. Tie the other end of the ribbon under the collar on the stick. Cover the knots with another piece of ribbon.

6 Decorate the Styrofoam ball by gluing on more ribbons and craft foam, and wind ribbon around the craft stick.

Did you know...
The Tudors' favorite jesters got to live and eat in the Royal Court.

make a
Tussie mussie

The Tudors used scented flowers and herbs to hide bad smells and keep away "bad air," which they thought carried diseases such as the **plague**. They pinned small, scented **posies** called tussie mussies to their clothes.

You will need:
- ✛ Small real or paper flowers and sprigs of lavender or rosemary
- ✛ Scissors
- ✛ Sticky tape and rubber band
- ✛ Aluminum foil
- ✛ Paper doily or coaster
- ✛ Ribbon or raffia

1 Cut the flower stem and sprigs to the same length. Gather them into a tight bunch with the flower at the center and secure with tape or a rubber band.

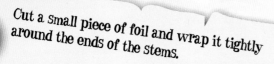

2 Cut a small piece of foil and wrap it tightly around the ends of the stems.

3 Cut a small hole in the center of the coaster or doily. Push the foil end of the posy through the hole.

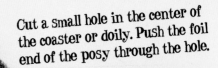

4 Gather the doily around the posy to form a collar and tape it in place.

5 Decorate the tussie mussie with trails of curly ribbon or raffia.

Did you know...

"Tussie" may come from a word meaning a knot of flowers, and "mussie" from the damp moss that was wrapped around them to keep them moist.

make a model of a Tudor house

In Tudor times, citizens' houses were built on **timber** frames with panels of "wattle" and "daub," which were made by smearing straw, mud, or animal **dung** onto twigs and branches. Black **tar** on the **beams** and **whitewashed** panels created the "half-timbered," or black and white, style.

You will need:
+ Three cardboard boxes
+ Glue and masking tape
+ Scissors
+ White acrylic paint
+ Sand
+ Brushes
+ Black construction paper
+ Marker
+ Poster board or card stock
+ Brown felt pen
+ Skinny craft sticks

1 Turn a box on its side and glue or tape it to another box to create an overhanging floor.

2 Cut and fold the third box to make a roof. Tape it in place on top of the boxes.

3 Mix a little sand into white acrylic paint and brush it onto the sides of the house. Allow it to dry.

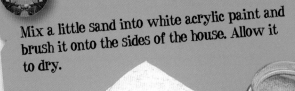

4 Cut strips of black paper and glue them onto the sides of the building to form the beams. Look at pictures of Tudor houses in books and on the internet to give you ideas.

5 Draw a door and some windows onto the card stock, cut them out, and stick them to the front of the building.

6 Glue skinny craft sticks onto the roof in overlapping rows to make a thatched roof.

Did you know...
Tudor houses were built with overhanging second stories. This gave them more room and let them avoid ground rent taxes!

make a Tudor ruff

Wealthy people in Tudor times wore frilled collars called ruffs, which were made from fine linen and lace. The ruffs could be washed separately from their clothes, and were starched and pressed by special **goffering irons**.

1 Fold the doilies into quarters to make cone shapes. Cut off the points.

2 Fold each sheet of paper widthwise to make a clean fold and then open it out again. Glue the doily edges along both long sides of each sheet of paper and allow to dry.

3 Make accordion folds backwards and forwards along each sheet of white paper, making each fold about 1 inch (3 cm) wide. Hold the pleats together and cut each sheet in half using a fold line as a guide.

4

Put the pleats together and punch a hole about 1 inch (3 cm) in from the edge of each section.

5

Glue the folded sheets together along the short edges to make a ruff long enough to fit around your neck, with 1 inch (3 cm) to spare.

6

Use the needle to thread the ribbon through the hole, then draw the ruff pleats together.

Did you know...

Some ruffs measured 12 inches (30 cm) across and needed wire frames to support them!

make a
Stained glass coat of arms

In Tudor times, **heraldic** badges or coats of arms showed who your family was or where you came from. Families displayed coats of arms on clothes, armor, shields and flags, and on the walls and windows of their houses.

You will need:
- ✚ Black construction paper
- ✚ Scissors
- ✚ Glue and sticky tape
- ✚ Red and blue cellophane
- ✚ Gold metallic paper

1 Fold a piece of black paper in half, and cut a half-shield shape along the fold line.

2 Keeping the shield shape folded in half, cut away a rectangle and a quarter circle, leaving a horizontal strip in the middle.

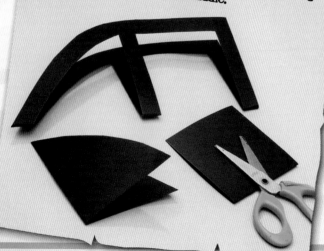

3 Open the shield shape up. Cut a strip of black paper and glue it onto the back down the middle to form four sections.

4

Cut a piece of blue cellophane and glue or tape it onto the back of two diagonally opposite sections. Repeat using red cellophane to complete the shield.

5

Cut two **fleur-de-lys**, or "flower of the lily," shapes (pictured right) and two Tudor roses (left) out of the gold paper. Glue one onto each section of the shield. Cut off any extra cellophane.

Did you know...
Rich Tudors sometimes had their family portraits painted onto glass windowpanes.

make a
Tudor cap

Hats were worn by people of all ages in Tudor times. The poor wore simple woolen caps, but rich men wore caps made from silk, velvet, or wool, often decorated with jeweled bands and feathers.

1 Draw two sets of circles on craft foam. The big circles measure 12 inches (30 cm) across. Inside the big circles, the small circles should measure 5 inches (13 cm) across. Cut out the big circles, then the small circles, so that you have two rings.

2 Cut out two circles of fabric measuring 5 inches (13 cm) wider than the foam rings. Staple one of the fabric circles to one of the foam rings to form the "crown" of the cap.

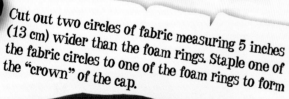

3 Snip around the edges of the other fabric circle. Cut out the center, and glue it to the second foam ring to form the "brim" of the cap.

4

Glue the crown of the cap to the brim.

5

Stick some gems to a piece of craft foam and cut out the shape to make a decorative badge.

6

Decorate the cap by gluing the feathers and the badge to the front.

Did you know...

A law in 1571 made all men and boys over six wear a woolen cap on a Sunday to help the wool trade!

make a
Ship's figurehead

Many ships in Tudor times had carved wooden **figureheads**. Traditionally, they were seen as the ship's eyes. Figureheads protected the ships, like good luck charms, and helped people identify each ship.

You will need:

+ Plastic spray bottle
+ Funnel
+ Sand
+ Aluminum foil
+ White glue and water
+ Tissue paper
+ String
+ Cardboard
+ Scissors
+ Acrylic and metallic paints
+ Brushes
+ Card stock
+ Red felt pen
+ Stapler

1 Remove the spray cap and make sure the bottle is clean and dry. Using the funnel, pour a little sand inside to add weight, then replace the cap.

2 Using the foil, mold the shape of a lion onto the bottle. Make oval shapes for the body and legs, and round shapes for the head, mane, and face. Secure the lion to the bottle with more foil.

3 Make papier-mâché by tearing tissue paper into strips and dipping them into a mix of equal parts white glue and water. Cover the figure in papier-mâché and leave it to dry.

4 Cut some short pieces of string and glue them in swirling shapes onto the papier-mâché to form the mane and fur. Cut a shield from cardboard and glue it to the front of the figure.

5 Paint your figurehead using acrylic paints. Use metallic paint to go around the shield and for the fur and claws. When it is dry, use black acrylic paint to paint the face.

6 Use the card stock to make a crown and the decoration for the shield, and then stick them to the figure.

Did you know...
The famous ship the *Mary Rose* had a Tudor rose for its figurehead.

make a
Cup and ball

Tudor children played with simple toys, often carved from wood. The cup and ball was a popular game of catch. Children swung the ball on a string into the air and tried to catch it in the cup.

Tape the bottom of the cup to one end of the cardboard tube.

Using the skewer or knitting needle, make a hole through the center of the Styrofoam ball.

Paint the cone and the ball two contrasting colors.

4

Decorate the cone, using masking or electrical tape to make stripes.

5

Cut a length of wool or string about 8 inches (20 cm) long and thread the needle. Push the needle through the hole in the Styrofoam ball and make a knot in the end of the string to hold it to the ball.

6

Make a hole in the cup and thread the other end of the string through it. Make a large knot inside to hold it firmly in place.

Did you know...
Other wooden toys included hoops, spinning tops, skittles, and rattles.

make a Tudor clothespin doll

Dolls in Tudor times were often made from scraps of fabric and wooden clothespins. Some were homemade and others were sold by traveling salesmen called peddlers.

1 Cut a circle of fabric, making the radius the same size as the height of the clothespin. Cut a small hole in the center.

2 Push the clothespin through the hole and glue the fabric onto it, leaving the top of the clothespin showing. Tie a piece of ribbon around the middle of the clothespin to secure the fabric and make a waist.

3 Cut a pipe cleaner in half and glue it onto the clothespin to make arms. Twist the ends to make small hands.

4

Draw a face onto the clothespin. Cut short pieces of wool and glue them on to make hair.

5

Cut a semicircle from some colorful fabric to make a cape or a jacket. Glue under the arms to hold it in place.

6

Make a ruff by making an accordion fold with a strip of white paper and gluing it to the doll's neck. Cut a piece of gold braid and glue it to the wool to form a hair band.

Did you know...
In Tudor times, dolls were known as "wooden babies."

Glossary

Apprentice A young person learning a skilled trade or craft.

Beam A length of wood, metal, or stone that supports a building or roof.

Carnival A type of festival or fair.

Dung Waste from animals.

Figurehead A carved wooden figure fixed to the front of a ship.

Fleur-de-lys, "flower of the lily" A three-petal representation of a lily.

Goffering iron An iron that is used to press folds or pleats.

Guild A group formed by people with the same job or skills.

Heraldic To do with the coats of arms of noble families.

Journeyman An assistant craftsman, sometimes hired by the day.

Linen A fabric made from a plant called flax.

Masquerade A dance at which guests wear masks and costumes.

Medieval From the Middle Ages, the period of history which lasted from about 1000–1500 CE.

Monarch A king or queen.

Navigation The science of finding your way at sea or on land.

Plague A deadly disease in Tudor times.

Portrait A painting of a person.

Posy A small bunch of flowers.

Reign The period of time that a king or queen rules for.

Royal Court The household that is centered on the king or queen.

Scepter A ceremonial staff carried by a monarch.

Symmetrical A design made of shapes that are mirror images of each other.

Tar A black, sticky substance mostly made from coal.

Timber Wood prepared for building.

Whitewash A mixture of lime and water, used to paint walls white.

Further information

BOOKS

Plague: The Black Death
Janey Levy
Gareth Stevens Publishing, 2015

Terrifying Tudors
Terry Deary and Martin Brown
Scholastic Press, 2016

The Tudors: Kings, Queens, Scribes, and Ferrets!
Marcia Williams
Candlewick, 2016

WEBSITES

PowerKids Press has developed an online list of websites related to the subject of this book. This site is updated regularly. Please use this link to access the list:

www.powerkidslinks.com/cb/tudors

Index